The Rasping Staircase Poems

Steve Baba

Crimson Milk Press
San Francisco

Cover design by Steve Baba

Ways to contact the author:
www.stevebaba.com
facebook.com/stevebaba
twitter.com/stevenhbaba

First printing, April 2015
Printed in the USA

ISBN:
ISBN-13:

Table Of Contents

I.

Shock Value 13
Oscar 14
On Fire 15
Contours 16
Ignite 17
Pitch 18
Vegas Sucks 19
A First Time For Everything 20
Pain And Joy 21
Likewise 22
Dog's Paws 23
Rebel 24
Marching Orders 25
Double Double 26
Collision 27
Surprises Galore 29
Trans-something 31
S Is For Sex 32
The PAIN! 34
Shadows, Ghosts 35
The Good Kind Of Crazy 36
Hey! 37
The Bad Kind Of Crazy 38
Rhyme Time 39
Outdoors 40
Ugly Is The New Buzzword 41
All Hail! 42
Bag o' Crap 43
Another Addict's Story 44
Pad Thai 45

He's All Business 46
The Last Of The Lot 47
For All The Authors Out There- Dead Or Alive 48

II.

The PAIN! Part Two 51
Lucky Or Unlucky? 53
Out And About 54
Drifting 55
For Kat Krippen 56
Summer And Winter Holidays 57
Frustrated 58
Just Another Summer Day 59
I'll Protect You 60
Is This Paris? 61
Cherries Scream 62
Lovers 63
Please Try 64
Lounging 65
Sexist 66
Leave Them Alone 67
Angus 68
Don't Forget To Chew 69
Firefly 70
Bastards 72
Had To Grow Up Sooner Or Later 73
Missing Hawaii 74
Shingles 75
Angels And Demons 76
He Follows My Every Thought 77
Stop Worrying 78
Europe Vs. Africa 79
Wrong Place, Wrong Time 80

Sensations 82
Burning Up 83
Don't Need Anything 84
Exclaim! 85

III.

Conveyor Belt 89
Incidents Happen 90
Childhood 91
Thinking About It 92
Survival 93
Labor And Delivery 94
Hallucinations 95
Midnight Kiss 96
Anniversary 97
The Truth 99
Hotel Shenanigans 100
Crazy Love 102
Death Comes Easily 103
White And Proud Of It 104
The End Of All Things 105
High School Memories 106
Beginning To Waver 107
My Comrade 108
The Hunt 109
I Thought So 110
Tangled Wire 112
First Girlfriend 113
Dissolving 114
Witness 115
The Coming Of Fall 116
Dead Man's Face 117
A Student Poet's Life 118

Confused 119
Argument 120
Was This Really Love? 121
Accident 122

IV.

Chocolate 125
Listen To The Voice 126
Hay 127
Time Remembers 128
Lightning 129
Not Ugly 130
Appearances Can Be Deceiving 131
Can It Be That Difficult? 132
Jack 133
Problems 134
The 20's 135
Adolescence 136
How Embarrassing- Paying For Sex 137

For Grandpa Baba

I.

Shock Value

i bought a whore
on 2nd and 5th
she was long legged
and beautiful

we went to a hotel
and got a room

you know
the ones that rent
by the hour

i carried the bottle of red wine
in my left hand

my right hand on her shoulder

we went into the room
and sat on the bed

this is my first time she said
this is my first time

we drank the wine
she undressed
and the bed became bruised
and broken

Oscar

grumbled the sun
there are too many clouds

grumbled the moon
there are too many stars

i asked if it was okay
to show my soft side

she said yes
i hugged her and told her
that i was not confused anymore

deep breaths
shining coin
breakfast served hot

the roses were beautiful
at last the petals were
falling to the ground

sitting on a dock
letting the water
caress my naked feet

i was a skyscraper
brushing heaven

On Fire

if she were a breath of wind
i would suffocate
because my eyes would catch
on fire

remember the templates
of love
i looked at them under a microscope
and saw attachment
detachment

pretty evergreen
you defy the winter
you carry the snow on your
strong limbs

pretty rose
you carry the smell of hope
when all is dark

i want to be a rock
under a wave of water
no remorse
no mercy

dream of the curly haired woman
who brought nourishment
to a heart that has been in a coal mine
for a thousand years

Contours

i am a giant
i step on ants
sleep on dewy grass

you are the rumble
in my stomach

the stars in my eyes

he took a picture
of the monster that
hid under his bed

hangnail
broken thumb
crooked index finger

hello
how are you?
it's cold outside

the deep creases in
his forehead
like contours on a map

Ignite

the deepest wound
is the mariana trench

the fish swim in the dark
and i swim naked with no reservations

as the swans follow the sun
into oblivion
i follow nobody

don't stop me
from eating a piece
of rope

i'll drink gasoline
until my stomach ignites

break the wood beam
over oiled knees

and wait for the boiling
of the skin on skin on face

stay behind the deuce
clasp the infinite negatives

Pitch

a tear of ink slowly
wafted down her cheek

her fingers black
her eyes black

the letter just finished
so hard to say goodbye

but she knew it was
for the best

what else were she to do?
keep on faking the inevitable?

he would have to pick
up the pieces

and he was good at that

but the cost in his heart
would be infinitely more
than the lightness in his wallet

she licked the envelope
and kissed it once

jet washed over it
gratitude not withstanding

Vegas Sucks

let's get back to it
the dice and dirty cigarettes

i'll pour the whiskey
you get your lips ready

for a kiss?
for the warm liquid that
dissipates dreams?

neither

i'm going to put a bullet on
your tongue
and you're going to swallow it

friends to the end
right?

A First Time For Everything

his face the color of
the sun

all he had to do is come out
and all would be well

instead he wore a gold ring
on his left hand
he cut his hair short

he even hid his lisp
that reverberated through the walls
when he was talking dirty

sashaying into the room
he wanted so much to show his penis
to him

but he smiled with duct tape lips
he grew up that night
when he was finally rejected

took the bait
and smoked the joint

he got high too quickly
and jumped off the diving board
into an empty swimming pool

Pain And Joy

my tooth hurts so bad
the nurses pass out when
they look in my mouth

skin crinkled like a
potato chip
salsa dancing on a piece
of plastic

they got married in hawaii
right after my grandma died
she was looking down
and thinking
this is a good day

door knobs in butter
a cherry towel from japan
don't touch youth

auntie gave me some money
a monet
and a medal from my deceased cousin

easy there
don't break your leg
like a cigarette being chopped
in two

empty bowls
water canister
did i gape at the shoe?

Likewise

twisted melded
a ripe banana peeled

carburetor slick
with ink

urine the color of
a ripe pear

eating raw pasta
the tooth chipped
and aching like
a hummingbird's wings

self doubt
the candy and vanilla tea
soothe the beast

gotcha
ol' bill will die
when the undertaker
puts him in the front
of his list

crabby person
be nice to children
or hell it is for your soul

conducive to laughing
i heard the joke 5 years ago
still funny

Dog's Paws

scratch the ink off the fingers
let the wood filter through your
nostril hairs

clear the throat
tale of a monk who
never sang
lost everything
lost everything

brush the flakes from
your shoulders
oh snow in august
smells like a british teen

reach out for the pickle
and stain it to the chair
break a shoe

the newspaper
was worn thin from
the dog's paws
glass glass glass

for one fear
you get one black licorice vine
for one hope
you get a shower of uranium

Rebel

her heart was seedy
and dimly lit

but that was what she
liked about her

daggers on her heels
razors for teeth

if the one thing she
hated were men
then why did she subscribe

to all those men's magazines?

she drove a honda accord
teal and with 25,000 miles on it

she ate oysters
with the pearls still inside

when she went to the bathroom
she sprayed perfume on her ass
just to make it smell good

31 days later
she wanted to get pregnant
so she went to the local
sperm bank

Marching Orders

the tedious shovel
eats the dirt until rocks
spark against it

runny nose
poor little kid
they hate him for that

bitter tongue
like someone lit a candle
on it

a bicycle that was
left behind
grease thick on the chain

clear the throat
play the music
toss the boxes into the trash

shoes not shiny
but dull brown
where are the marching orders?

stop it
stop it right now
my fingers feel like stalagmites

down comforter
please stop shedding like
a cat in summertime

Double Double

slowly slowly
the guitar strummed
and patient

forget forget
the belly protruding
and large

deem deem
the love of one another
and satisfied

catch catch
not a cold but a stone eye
and seeing not much

hope hope
for the greatest laugh
and milk sprayed from the nose

great great
of caesar you are the best
pooh pooh on brutus

box box
the meth and smoke it soon
and you'll die like a fly

satisfy satisfy
the urge to dance
and shoes shine in the ballroom

Collision

the stoplight didn't turn
green and everyone was angry

as the truck went into the intersection
a small child walked into the street

when the truck stopped
the driver knew he had hit something

he got out and saw the bloodstains
on his wheels

they cried out
all of them
why? why? why?

the driver took a handkerchief and
wiped his brow

then the sirens came
and they got louder and louder
as the voices got angrier

little richard was 8 years old
and he had just learned how to paint

little richard was 8 years old
and he had just memorized
a poem for his mom on this day

valentine's day
when the noise stopped
everyone held their breath

when the truck moved
everyone hid their eyes

little richard was 8 years old
and he died a senseless death
at the hands of a man who had
whiskey on his breath
and death in his eyes

but he did not die
it was poor richard
whom would be buried at dawn
next to grandma and grandpa

Surprises Galore

his teeth like
icing on a cake

soon he would have to
get those teeth
changed into ceramic

the wrists ache
because she took his hand
way too many times

the knees curl in pain
because she would always
scratch at them

a gap
a missed shoe
a braid of red hair

there it is
the lost idea
and now since he
didn't write it down

he lost it again

sneezes
gagging on liver
twitching eyelid

oh how i know it all
if not now when?

probably tomorrow
if i'm still kicking

Trans-something

i don't have a vagina
but i wanted one
in the worst way

once when i went to
the bathroom

i mistook diarrhea
for piss

when i was small
i told my grandpa that
i wanted one

he said do you want to
cut off your penis?

i thought for a second
and then said no

but i envied the women in
my family

how cool that you could put
something inside you

how cool that you could hide
things in there

S Is for Sex

don't force it
you'll blow an o ring
if you do

don't grip on too tight
or it will turn purple

don't put your fingers
in too far
or it will hurt

don't suck too softly
or it will tickle

foreplay
what's that?

just stick it in and have
a grand old time

just remember to pull out
before the end
or you'll suffer the consequences
9 months later

on the sofa
on the table
in bed

it doesn't matter where
as long as we are as pink
as flamingos

The PAIN!

my stomach won't leave
me alone

it is rummaging through the
acid bath and it finds nothing
so it bellows loud and clear

my fingers ache
i chewed on them last night
with my dirty teeth

shy that way?
yes i was
and still am

astonished to hear that
picasso died in the 70's
he was a damn good painter

please stop the runny nose
or i'll take your picture

dan was a good man
a gay man
with a bald head
and lucky breath

as the world sleeps
as the world wakes up
as the world lives its life

Shadows, Ghosts

the ghosts of yesterday
still haunt this place

they disguise themselves
as bed sheets
as a shower curtain

they cannot speak
as their tongues have
been cut out

they eat the mothballs
they drink the mold

when it is midnight
that is when they
become alive

her mother just couldn't
let go

she resisted the light
and stayed in the material world

her dad couldn't let her mom
be by herself so
he stayed behind too

and little bobby
who died of tuberculosis
he still wanted to play

The Good Kind Of Crazy

my left eye itches today
i wonder if it's the pollen
or something else

elephant trunk
a glass full of beads
he said goodbye to the undertaker

a pack of cigarettes
lasts for 12 hours
and then the drooling comes

she opened a can of pickles
with her breast
so firm so tight

at last the sun touched the
moon
but only on a day that felt
so incongruent

wash the soap from the mouth
eat the lentils
take out the garbage

when oh when will it
be my time lord?

i am so tired i can sleep
on a bed of hot coals

\
Hey!

the blue vein on your breast
is still as large as your nipple

mexican music plays on the radio
ice melts onto your cheeks

dance why don't you?
do the salsa

the mucus is blocking your
breathing in your nose

cough up a diamond
this time it didn't cost you
two paychecks

ah bladder
you're full of poison

let it go
let it go

hello butterfly
land on my shoulder
and give me a kiss

The Bad Kind Of Crazy

a bump
an itch
a cry in the night

a chocolate bar
a love song playing on the radio
sweat covering her face

glasses
fogged up
i just want to say

trucks and cars
fly by
golden coin in the hand

blankets
pillows
a baby's soft head

time to confess
that you didn't do it
that she was the one with
the knife

earplugs
silence
and a sugar cookie

Rhyme Time

orange glue
windbreaker shoes

i saw the goat chewing
and i realized that it could
be raining right now

my thumbnail black
i broke it on a friday night
and someone ate my kite

tongue tastes like snot
the slime makes it harder
to breathe in real air

she was always wobbly
and i thought hey
why don't i drink that too

her large brown eyes
the size of silver dollars
i want to creep into her bra

never be alone
as i always say
that's a lie and will always be

Outdoors

pretty cardinal
why don't you find a mate?

willow tree
why don't you finally
fall asleep?

the books on the shelf
are gathering dust

my friend says that i need
to read them before i die

i said i want another
pour of whiskey

the rotten watermelon
is all dried out and fuzzy

my friend says i should have
eaten it

i said i want another
piece of chocolate cake

Ugly Is The New Buzzword

he preached abstract
he practiced concrete

when he carried that
book around
people were impressed

his booming voice
making even the bravest
child scared

but he smelled like a sewer
he looked like a demon

bought a ticket to kalamazoo
to sample the coffee

lake michigan in the background
with a few ugly birds
flying around the frigid air

his teeth were the color of corn
his eyes the color of a sharpie

death was never brought up
because his mom died when she
was in labor with him

All Hail!

if i were to tell you
that you were going to die

i think you would ignore me

if i were to tell you
that you would get rabies

you would let the cat bite you

101 degrees
on your neck
the mouse scampers
into the open closet

9 mosquito bites
like someone was playing
connect the dots

his hair gone now
where is the justice?
i wanted him to be good

swing the chalice into the air
and watch it fall into the mind
goodbye babe ruth

Bag O' Crap

the bamboo is ready to eat
why does he have so much gas?

the table is set for dinner
why is his colostomy bag upset?

she thought she would take her
face and dab it with fire
then she could handle the thought
of killing herself

the egrets flew by
a pelican circled overhead
one robin's egg ready to hatch

caught between the life
of a nun
or the life of a whore

she liked sex
but was scared more of god
and so she shaved her head
and moved to rome

the great price of sugar
is almost free now

Another Addict's Story

the needle pins itself
into his limp arm
the shock makes his
blue eyes white

then the medicine goes in
he gasps once
and falls to his knees

the stars seem so far away
the moon hidden this night

the needle pulls out
and a dab of red
replaces the small wound

he closes his eyes
and thinks of sugar

why sugar?
why not a nipple?

he stands up and breathes in
the dirty night air

the ears are buzzing
i thought bees went to sleep
when it got dark

Pad Thai

rub the juice
of the mulberry
into your eyes

you will see the
ancients looking
at you

when the pad thai
of your life
is served on a hot plate

you will feel a burn
in your stomach
that is unbearable

come into the light
and watch the water
flow through rocks

i am a doctor
with no cure for
what ails you

fly on the wall
infect the air
with your petty virus

He's All Business

the man in the suit
knows nothing but money

his wallet full of credit cards
his briefcase full of important documents

when he rides in the taxi
all he thinks of is how far he
can get ahead

then a homeless man
comes to his window
he asks for a few coins

the man makes a face of disgust
he pinches his nose
he cringes

the tie on that man
is tight around his throat

i wonder if he knows that
will be the death of him

or maybe jumping out of his
30th floor office window

The Last Of The Lot

tiger skin
eel bites
a solemn soldier
eats a pear

salami mind
honey teeth

caterpillar scab
broken sun

musical fan
gaseous rocks

she took a knife
and stabbed it into
a hapless pillow

cordial afro
remote itch

there is a place
where you can forget
the most worrying
of crazy people

For All The Authors Out There- Dead Or Alive

crimson tide
the waves of heat
break on the summer days

twinkling eyes
cold soda makes
the throat wet

bright star
i find you in the
night skies until
the sun comes up

ten more hours
and i will be sober

five more months
and new york
is calling to me

eyebrows raise
no breath too spicy

too weird
the ants eat the
dead cockroach

II.

The PAIN! Part Two

my bladder hurts
spikes and rocks
rattle in it

my nose hurts
needles in vessels
scratch and get a waterfall

my chest hurts
why the hammer?
why the caltrops?

he walked along the seine
and wanted to jump in

not to drown himself
but to see if his skin would
melt off

a gaslight still on
after the sun came up
if it exploded they would
have thought it were a rocket
going into space

my eye hurts
twitch twitch
sponges and darts

my feet hurt
rolling rolling
on the hot coals

my stomach hurts
rock a bye baby
spurt spurt

she caught a cockroach
sifting through her sugar
wham! wham!
no more cockroach

he realizes knees
that creak

that fingers curl
that wrists burn

but the no man's land
hasn't been touched in
55 years

Lucky Or Unlucky?

she gazed at me with
dollar bills in her eyes

she put her arm in mine
and said i was lucky

by the hour
or by the night

we walked down the
wet sidewalk
but i wasn't interested

i let go of her arm
and said
maybe another time

now i saw coal in her eyes
she whispered something
you must be gay

i kept on walking
and then another woman
came to me

this time with 50 dollar
bills in her eyes

i sighed and walked right past her
tonight was not a good night

Out And About

garbage in
garbage out

the cantina plays jazz
so sweetly
even the prostitutes cry

goats congregate on the
steep mountainside

i see a robin
landing in its nest
3 eggs

five in the morning
the coffee brewing
the newspaper hits
the front door

the face scalded in
hot water

the screams of the children
silenced by the black hole
that has formed in their beds

Drifting

this here's jake
he hears voices

and andy
he fought in vietnam

sally was a cook
in a five star restaurant

they like warm manholes
they eat what people throw away

one day a policeman came
to make jake move away

he took out his baton
and struck jake on his left forearm

jake kicked at the policeman
and then the policeman drew his gun

plug plug
poor jake

he was a good guy

For Kat Crippen

i recorded a bratwurst while
she pierced my ear

blue hair
a lot of smiles
and captivating brown eyes

oh kat
you make me think
of strawberries and cream

oh kat
i saw that you
were kind to other people

the puzzle goes on though
what is the meaning of bottle caps?

forget the alcohol
take the top apple

faking a bad temper
just so i can say
i was mad at you once

Summer And Winter Holidays

the scab on his arm itched
that damn mosquito

the bags under his eyes
were as black as coal

the lines in his smile
so genuine

he ate a piece of apple pie
and savored each bite

where are the children?
are they outside?

the football game was boring
neither team had a winning record

the glass of red wine
still cool

a mouse scampered across
the kitchen

a drop of water landed
into the sink

Frustrated

thumb broken
i'm not going to see
her anymore

she disappeared
the day i hit the wrong nail

i will be at the lake
she told me
that morning

i fixed all the holes
i fixed all the problems
but with you
i would never be able to fix

when they found your body
i was like a hailstorm
i was like a torrential downpour

that thorn in your heart
is finally plucked out

that steel band
removed from your head

Just Another Summer Day

the heat was terrific
that late august afternoon

she drank some ice water
and scratched at the bite
on her knee

a fly buzzed right by
her ear
and landed on her nose

she swatted it away
a drop of sweat came down

the man that walked by her
said she was pretty

she smiled
and waved to him

a woman in a sweatshirt
walked by with a baby carriage

the baby's blue eyes
sparkled like marbles
at her

I'll Protect You

rest your weary head
on my lap

i won't let the razors
or scissors get you

let's look under the bed
in the closet

see? no monsters
only air and dust

maybe he will come visit you
in the middle of the night

don't be afraid
he just wants to be
your friend

i'll open the window
you can gaze at the moon
and stars

let them help you fall
asleep when your mind
is full of angry wasps

Is This Paris?

aching back
let the beer
soothe the twitching muscles

i smell dirty
it's on the ground
between hot and cold

off to paris
picasso's ghost
still striding in the
streets

i went to the select
and had a cappuccino
the newspaper on my lap

rain came down
and made the air as crisp
as a fresh red apple

the bridge
with a thousand locks
had my love on
the fence

Cherries Scream

it doesn't matter
gold tooth stuck in traffic
stove dropped from cigar smoke

it's okay now
cherries scream at the strawberries
she speaks in time and space

it was a joke
i'm not laughing
i'm not smiling

spic and span on the waterfront
sailor makes garbage
and you must leave this atmosphere

shake it up
shake it up
shake it up

there's that hole in the star
where all is lost
book tries to creep away

wonder why?
because god said emeralds
because satan said habanero

Lovers

when i see couples
holding hands
it makes me feel like
a microwave oven on high

we met so long ago
we thought it wasn't
going to last

but look at us now
we are here still holding
each other's hands

the hair on the back of
my neck always rises up when you
kiss me

brown eyes
just like the silt from
the bottom of a clear stream

you told me to come to you
you wouldn't cause any wounds
you wouldn't love me less

like a christmas tree lit up
that's my heart
that's my heart

Please Try

i'm tired
i'm so tired

of hearing your shit
of hearing my shit

why can't we just look
at each other and be happy?

laughter was always my intention
and you laughed

to know more about you
to learn more about myself

that there will be good times
they will come to us in time

i smile to myself
and think that this is it
the happiest time of my life

you the cherry tree
full of cherries

me the water
giving you nourishment

don't be so cautious
be open
be alive

Lounging

they say that the mountains
will be in the sea

how long it will take
they do not know

they say the forests will
turn into desert

how long it will take
they do not know

i took a sip of water
when the clock saw
that the sun was in the middle
of the sky

and i walked along the
miniskirts and bikinis

i thought i was in heaven
so this is what muslims think about
when they blow themselves up

i shake my head
and take a bite of a chocolate
chip cookie

don't be afraid
don't be afraid

Sexist

when he talked about her
it sounded like a trashy novel

she with the torn nylons
kiss me lipstick
and cleavage

he would tell them
that she was his
always always

and that she was a good
woman who would cook and
clean and raise babies

but then she walked in
and she was all but what he said

she was tall
with long thick legs

long blonde hair put up
in a ponytail

she had a severe face
as if a storm had covered the
windshield with ice

and that voice
it sounded like horns blaring
in a traffic jam on 5th avenue

Leave Them Alone

beg for the money
beg for the food

he was a war veteran
of 20 years

the signs of age
wore on his face like
an unremovable mask

his hands like
barbed wire

his body felt like
a punching bag

he wandered the streets
trying to remember his
beloved's name

it escaped him
he would be alone for
the rest of his life

Angus

just a moment alone
that's all i want

like standing behind
the curtain
while they announce you
and the girl next to you

as prom queen and prom king

i don't wear masks
i only wear tired shoes
and my smile
it is the real thing

i took that ring off a long time ago
and my heart walks on the sidewalk
with me
as i see the jungle

cupid
you fool
i cannot be swayed easily
with an arrow

but for her
it is the tide coming in
it is the tulips in full bloom

Don't Forget To Chew

please take that diaper
and burn it in the abyss
the smell is like a rotten
piece of meat

take the dagger and stab the cheese
put it in that hole
and don't forget to chew

the strings in my arms
are waiting for the sharp pain
and then bliss
and then bliss

half a toenail
bitten off by a goat
he liked it so much
he ate part of my foot

a refund for the return of
my heart
you emptied it like my
scum ridden pool

priority comes to those
who beg for water
the desert is a dry birthday cake

shoelace
woodpecker
a paper written with urine

Firefly

callouses on my mind
where is the broken mirror?

the apricots have fallen
off the tree

my tongue is raw from
tasting the bitterness of life

my hands touched god
when i dreamt of her
holding me in the coming twilight

the door is open
the locks unlocked
the light is on

fingers rub the temple
the headache of love
will not subside

bring the robin
to its nest

take the acorn
and plant it

there will be no more
sadness this afternoon

as the sunlight
shines like a firefly
in my eyes

Bastards

he told her about the cats
the unlucky ones that were
to be eaten by chinese men
with expensive suits
and american express cards

a y shaped pole
was used to strangle the cat

and it was then dipped in
a vat of boiling oil
for 30 seconds

as the cat tried to breathe
the cat was lifted out
and its fur scraped off

then it was put into a
cauldron of cold water
still trying to breathe

a hammer to the head
and it went limp

so that's what they do to cats
in china
she said

and she threw up her angel cake
on the polished dining room table
unable to fathom what had just
been discussed

Had To Grow Up Sooner Or Later

pick up that piece of pie
and eat it right now!

you kill it
you eat it
no excuses

(this told from a father
to his son when the son
killed a robin with his slingshot)

wash your hands
or you will taste soap

clean up your room
or the toes that are clean
will end up like your room

so this is why we
end up so messed up
and parents wonder why

we are anorexic
we are suicidal
we turn to drugs

if they had one word of kindness
in their mouths
maybe we wouldn't be
coughing up anger

Missing Hawaii

besos to my
smooth faced one
don't look back

together the stars
will gather the tears
and shower them
down on us

today i was thinking
whether i was going to
stay or leave

one time i thought
about a pikake lei
she put it on me
that was 7 years ago

been leaving the bread
out in the open
no wonder it gets moldy

stop it
stop it now
i want to be happy
so don't take my hair
and burn it

Shingles

knives knives knives
jack-o'-lantern
a spoonful of sugar

headache
feather pillow
conductor of heat

despair
you've always been there
no fear no fear

nothing is real
except for the heart
it still shatters everyday

bird
why do you mock me?

sylvester was on steroids
he never lied about it
be good hayley

wasted chicken
no diseases
except for shingles

Angels And Demons

an angel floats
up into the sky

i am confused

was he icarus
back from the dead
so he could
really fly?

was he my grandpa
making an unscheduled visit
to see me and make sure
i was doing alright?

was it the devil in disguise
trying to make me believe
that my life is not worth anything?

i don't know
and i have this feeling
that i will never know

glass houses
crimson meteor showers
the dust in the corner

when she speaks
it will be like a violin
playing in a concert

He Follows My Every Thought

i have not felt this way
in a hundred days now

the despair running from
my mouth to my stomach

like ink flowing down an arm

i swallow and feel a rock in
my throat

where are the angels now?

the pitched fork
pokes me in the side

the heat is unbearable
but still i do not sweat

black eyes
stare at me

you are mine
you are mine

beneath the surface
there is a tearing wind that
takes away hope

that takes away love

Stop Worrying

the other day
i remembered how
ice cream tasted for
the first time

the cold sweetness
the crunchy cone

there was an earthquake
in indonesia yesterday

no tsunami
no tsunami

i hadn't taken a shower
in several days

i wanted her touch to feel
like whiskey burning in
my stomach

need a haircut
need to trim my nails
need to stop worrying

spicy scent
go away
i don't want to smell
you anymore

Europe Vs. Africa

flutes showed him
that music was something
he could appreciate

but the drums sounded
and the african natives
were ready to kill him

he walked along the seine
and saw the moon and stars
hiding in the ripples

the cigarette glowed
like a lighthouse in fog

he smashed the spent butt
into the ground
like a man beating another man
into oblivion

then he saw a beautiful prostitute
leaning against a bridge
she with depressing black eyes

he walked up to her and
put his arm around her stone shoulder

you shouldn't be out here tonight
you should be at home with the children

Wrong Place, Wrong Time

boldly she went to the market
by herself

she walked
telling herself she would
never take the bus ever again

it was a hot and humid day
that day

luckily she wore her
two year old tennis shoes

when she got to the market
there were a couple of young men
smoking cigarettes

they watched her with the devil
in their eyes

she bought her groceries
and left with a smile

the young men followed her
on foot

she didn't notice them
because her mind was on the
weight of the paper bags
and the sweat on her brow

they sneaked up on her
threw her groceries to the ground
threw her to the ground

they stripped her naked
and then ravished her

there you go
they said after they finished

now you'll have some white
in your life

Sensations

vicious teeth
don't bite me
don't clasp onto
my loose skin

the taste of butter
has disappeared from my tongue
all i taste is ash

she was going to
bring me happiness

all i got was
the smell of rotten apples
in my nose

catch the wind
stir the leaves
feel the cold on the cheeks

so sorry
i was an idiot
trying to learn calculus

so sorry
i was ignorant
to your calls of help

Burning Up

shave the dirty face
volcano heart
look to the favorite
son bringing home
his bride

poof!
the poem is eviscerated
red balloons
hover in the sky

calmer calmer
cigarettes fly in
the hands
smoke brought to you
by camel

look to the nickel
with the blank face
they were made without care
and the mint got punished

Don't Need Anything

when i feel like
veronica
i stop and say

i don't need anything

roasted chicken
new potatoes
a glass of chardonnay

a jacket
a t-shirt
socks
pants
boxers

no rain can come in
quiet prevails

i have a blessed woman
whom i fell in love with
3 years ago

she is a marisa tomei
a georgia o'keefe
a jane kenyon

Exclaim!

whew!
the makeup didn't run

sigh!
her smile was upside down

cough!
too many cigarettes

meh!
i don't know why

blech!
it tastes like charcoal

i like it when you
press your lips against
the glass

i like it when you
become a pretty woman

III.

Conveyor Belt

she smiled when the
baby came out of her

her breasts tingled
the nipples ready for that
hungry mouth

the doctor made sure
she was alright

no more blood
no more amniotic fluid

when she held him in
her arms
he looked like elvis

when she touched his face
his flesh quivered
in the pale light

sleep sleep
eyes and bags
like suitcases on a
conveyor belt

Incidents Happen

apple elevator
fan that talks to strangers

she hummed that song
the one you hated
she still did it anyways

crash the gums
die mouse die!

the ship was sinking
and the captain was the
first man to disembark

what a coward

drinks on me
drinks on me
nothing seems the same
except for the blue
contacts that you wear now

help yourself to the soup
i'm done with it
don't let the flies get into it

Childhood

his mind is empty
of all the pain he suffered
when he was a boy

that cigarette burn scar
told him to not forget the fear
of his father

mom worked nights
the drunken fights
and he was always the winner

a broken television
a spilled glass of beer
and the used condom

he was all muscles
by the time he was in high school
those weights did wonders

but that man
he would not stop
until he had a bat in his hand

when he died
there were only bones
just like he wanted it

Thinking About It

eyes like rain drops
slowly winding down the window

i have to tell you this
i have to tell you this

my stomach may be empty
my mind pre occupied
my face in a frown

but inside
deep inside my chest
i have decided to give that
to you

and i know you will lock it away
in that wood trunk filled with
your childhood toys

safe safe safe
20 years later
and it still looks new

you hold it in your hands
kiss it once
and throw it into the air

it turns into a beautiful cardinal
and flies away

Survival

they say because you're gay
you don't belong here

they throw stones
they insult
they try to rip it from your soul

but you have always been good
good to your family
good to your neighbors
good to your friends

they say you are abomination
that you will burn in hell

you loved her so much
she was your best friend
she was your love of your life

when she kissed your breasts
it felt like the sun shining on them
for the very first time

you will endure
you will triumph
you will still tolerate humankind

Labor And Delivery

he bought a new car
a red corvette

he hoped it would hide
the bald spot on his head

she was pregnant
with twins
she hoped it would

make her marriage stick

as she went into labor
her husband grimaced for her

the babies were stillborn
two more lives she had taken

a dollar bill
a scoop of vanilla ice cream
some chocolate droppings in the cookies

dan was a good man
but this was too much
so he dropped the camcorder
and left the hospital

Hallucinations

the doughnuts
sit on the counter
waiting for the flies
to impregnate them

at 2 am
i screamed
that i wanted a glass
of bourbon

you shuffled on the wood floor
and silently poured it

at 5 am my eyelids
were sewn shut
with steel wire

and that dream
the one where you are
stepping in dog shit
at the gare du nord

right now
i just want a soft pancake
and some maple syrup

right now
i just want a doughnut
without the flies

Midnight Kiss

i ate a granny smith
while watching cnn

the weatherperson
was talking about another
drop in temperature

winter has finally come
the ice will form on windshields

i decided that it wouldn't
be winter

so i turned up the heat in the house
and took off all my clothes

ah now it feels like summer
with the dust emoting from the heater

with the sweat forming on my
upper lip and forearms

she always kissed like it
was midnight

all dark
all wet
all tough

Anniversary

i didn't know a bird
could be sad
but i saw it

when it flew over boston
the ground like a grave
red splotches everywhere

it went south to new york
and their hearts were hurting too

the center
was crying its tears

as a young boy
fell and didn't get up

they rose up
and helped the mighty
and the weak

the smoke lifted
and there was noise
noise everywhere

some lost limbs
others still critical

but today we saw some more heroes
and even though we will
probably forget them later

that bird will not forget
even when it lays eggs
and has children of its own

The Truth

i'm tired of you
i am not listening to
both sides of the story

cat meows
dog barks
a fish swims left to right

ingrown hair
red spots on the neck

the truth is there
i just know it

the eyes of that man scare me
he is looking at that woman
as if she were a broiled steak

peeling
scarred
unfortunate

the garbage can is full
of dead rats

the flies congregate
at the stuff on top

Hotel Shenanigans

at the hotel
the concierge brought
you the tickets to the opera

he winked at you
knowing you would give him
what he wanted that night

you went to the bar in the hotel
and ordered a whiskey straight up

the poor business man was
making a fool of himself
drooling all over the prostitute
who squeezed a couple drinks out of him

you finished your drink
and went to the lobby

where was she?
did she forget?
did she dust him off?

she finally did show
at the front of the hotel
with a mink coat
and lipstick as red as bloodshot eyes

the cab came
you both got into it
and then the sound of splashing
as the cab's wheel ran into a puddle

Crazy Love

when the sun came down
from its perch
it took one last look at the sky
before it headed west

the moon came out
and it was like a lightning bolt
from the heavens

like a maiden with
a see through gown
it went about its business
keeping people alive

just like its brother
it was a light that was the
end of all lights

it shared the sky
with stars

those pesky things
always blinking
never kissing

Death Comes Easily

the betrayal was complete
when she sent him the letter
that said she was to die tomorrow

the axe will fall
and her head will fall
into the empty wicker basket

today she will eat
a piece of chicken
a bowl of noodles
and drink some vintage red wine

her dress will be torn into
pieces
they will see her
white

whips
chains
bracelets made of steel

i feel sorry for her
because i know what
it's like to be tortured

White And Proud Of It

he banged the gun
against his chest

we will win!
we will win!

he touches the swastika
on his left arm
and smiles

they will leave!
they will leave!

he stubs out the cigarette
into the damp ground

the confederate flag
waves in the air
in defiance of the law

he tears out the pictures
of the black people in the magazine

sets it afire
in a small hole

he lifts up his chin
and runs his finger across his throat
as the chinese girl walks past him
to go to school

The End Of All Things

she hid from the mirror
lest she break it with her fists
those scars would never go away

she left leftover chinese
in the refrigerator
for 3 weeks

until the stench nauseated the cats

she piled the magazines
all the way up to the ceiling

never read
never read

when she opened the front door
she hid from the sun
like a vampire

when she walked in silence
in the night
she worried she would get raped

but her angel kept her safe
that is
until the last day of the year

she would have a stroke
and nobody knew

High School Memories

i was an elephant
when i was in high school

i was a jackal on the
soccer field

i was a bolt of lightning
on the baseball diamond

when my lesbian teacher
looked at me i tried to catch her eye

my classmates always liked me
even though i never had a girlfriend

i had two friends
one played chess
the other ate twinkies

we would hang out at lunch
trading stories of funny movies we saw

then it was june 1989
i barely made it through history class
my teacher gave me a d

and sitting on that bench as the
principal read my name
i felt like an unpeeled orange

Beginning To Waver

the hot noonday sun
beat its fists on his bald head
as he smoked a camel unfiltered

the stain on his shorts
the only evidence that he
loved his penis most

he took a sip from the
soda can
and spit

there on the sidewalk
a child's drawings
he used to do that when he
was a little boy

he put his arm up
into the air
the flies started to gather

a single drop of sweat
ran down his forehead
and into his left eye

that was the only way
he knew how to live
stay up and clap the audience

My Comrade

rest easy
my comrade

the red will
go away soon

i believe that
the sky will bring
diamonds
will bring gold

don't cough
don't sneeze
but smile widely

leave the cows alone
pick only a few cherries
walk on the carpet when
it dries

raw eggs
pierce the throat
raw almonds
chase the squirrels away

The Hunt

when the cherry tomato
sun goes down past the mountains
ice forms on my mustache

when the half moon comes out
i see the smoky stars
blink madness in the night

you cold hand
you cold foot

break the bones
of your enemies
with the butt of your shotgun

clear your throat
and let the candy
slip in and out of your tongue

the stomach aches for comfort
from the xenon gas
that coats the lining

i'm a deer that is afraid
of the sudden sounds
that come from the steps
of the hunter

I Thought So

he called and called
but nobody picked up

his bike was still against the wall
and it was lonely

tap tap
the walls are thin
he hears her snoring

the laughter has died
and she knows in her dreams
that his death will
be a violent one

invasion invasion
a body lying on the floor
a single drop of blood
on his cheek

the train stopped on the
last destination
he was to get off without
his pride

they waited
until there was a crowd
just so they would know
what they could do to someone

good luck they whispered
amongst themselves
even the police avoided the situation

Tangled Wire

taste the bark
of an oak tree

you will finally
know what bitter is

touch the sky
with your limpid eyes

it will shed its tears
it will bring warmth
to your achy bones

dollars
cents
a money order

no soap for this
filthy person

no shampoo
for the tangled wire
of hair on his misshapen head

cough cough
blankets cover cold toes

First Girlfriend

i was short
she was tall

she had an airplane strip
i was the jungle

when we walked
people gave us rude stares

this was the 90's
so what?

a quiet leaf in her hair
the ocean in her eyes

the first time we made love
we were both awkward
since it was our first time

the color of whiskey in her cheeks
a lark landing on her finger

we had a bad breakup
so bad i drank for a month straight

but when it was over
at least it was over

and not those stupid lingering things
where you have post relationship sex
and all that nonsense

Dissolving

greasy hair
chapped neck

it wasn't as heavy as
it looked

he put it on the ground
and walked away slowly

after 35 minutes it happened
bone skin and joints
all in a mess

she cried out for help
but nobody answered

the ground drank up
the blood

the ground smelled
of acid and burn

one eight year old child dead
his bladder still full

windows windows
cracked or shattered

Witness

we must stay alive
to witness the judgment
of the ones who wronged us

they will never be tortured
they will never be harassed
they will never lose heart

but when i stamp the ground
they'll be under me
wishing that they didn't do
what they did

when the walls crumble
i will be there
to see the bright light on the other side

when the ocean slows
and lets the tiny waves
lick the sand

i will put my feet in
and cleanse the dirt that they
have been putting inside of me
for so long now

The Coming Of Fall

when the wind makes
a swirl into the dead leaves
i feel disconcerted

happy days
have left in a huff

the sun no longer warms me
not even chocolate
makes me feel better

she has been gone a long time now
in a faraway land

i can't even see her in my mind
a murkiness has replaced her

the water that i drink
should be arsenic

my bowels
feel like a bomb has
gone off in them

where i'll go
i don't know
it will be on an island
where only goats reside

Dead Man's Face

she was as close to him
like the water to the sand

it was funny
because he always made
faces when she smiled at him

now his mouth slumps
because she's so far away

the breeze is freezing
the water now ice
and the sand so stiff

he walks into the water
and looks down
no feet
just seaweed and silt

he looks to the horizon
and feels human again
as the sun goes down and disappears

the bite on his arm
is as big as an apple
as big as a peach
but the color of a dead man's face

A Student Poet's Life

pick the one
you like the most

the blue one?
good

i would have finished my
meal of steak and potatoes

but my stomach
won't cooperate

skin
rocks
books

i like it when the
leaves leave for another
place

where they'll go
i'll never know

the bus is here
time to go to school
and i'll read dickinson at lunch

Confused

when the grass
turns yellow
you know it's summer

when the bleached clouds
move swiftly away
you know it's windy

stones piled up on the beach
a single child splashing in the water
that sunset that made you sin

he told me that he was black
not african american
and he knew it

i was not white
i was not yellow
i was not with slanted eyes

but i knew what it meant to
be oppressed

it was the god like cow
that made me stop eating meat

half smile
you betray my thoughts

Argument

the argument lasted
until dawn

broken mirrors
broken cups

she found out
and you made her cry

you tightened your belt
and tied your shoes

your wallet barely
staying in your back pocket

the gas leaks
the oil drips
cigarette smoke lingers
on the front porch

that drive was the longest drive
you ever took
to the beach

as the sun came over the mountains
you felt rain on your cheeks

Was This Really Love?

blink a stone
blink two
blink three
blink four stones
blink five
blink six

you'll not notice them
rolling down soon enough

your heart was a light bulb
it turned on when i touched you

your skin
like ripples of water
in the lake
when the moon is full

i want to keep you close
so the monsters don't eat you

i want to kiss you
honey
sugar
red apples

Accident

i saw a car accident
the other day

the ford truck
ran into an audi

i think the stoplights weren't
working because
they were both going the
same speed

a little girl
had blood in her
long blonde hair

a man had a cut from
his forehead to his cheek

glass on the ground
dented metal
but no lives lost

when the ambulance came
it was as loud as a trumpeting
elephant

they took away that little girl
and the man

the mother walked away unscathed
but with bourbon on her breath

IV.

Chocolate

when i saw the bright sun
blinding me
i felt like a tired old man
walking on his last walk

when i saw her lightly
kissing the air
i felt like a young man
who was a virgin

my face must have looked
like a jigsaw puzzle

my body sculpted
by rodin

but the day was a long one
i think it was june 21st

and i knew that if I had just waited
a little longer
she would be there

a good time
for having chocolate in my mouth

a good time to have a bottle
of champagne
in my hand

Listen To The Voice

the frog
jumped off the rock
and into the whirlpool

scum covered the water
vatos stabbed an elderly man
popsicles cost 50 cents

i am no good
he said
as he pulled the hair
of his five year old daughter

pus forms in the pimple
the thousand scars on her heart
always ache when it gets cold

slurp the chicken soup
hot hot hot
mice ramrod the garbage can

fan on
heat off
i am a perfect example
how not to enjoy life

Hay

if i had listened to you
that would be me
lying there in the dirt

if i had heard your cry
that would be me in the
clutches of that bald eagle

teeth smell like onions
breath like a dog after
it has licked itself

very good
mr. goose
you found the chocolate

speak louder
my hearing is a little rusty
lick the fruit wallpaper

strawberry
a discolored dime
hay stacked high in
the barn

that's what it feels like
when you miss someone

i won't tease at
dances ever again

Time Remembers

when love came my way
i rejected it
like a new kidney
rejecting its host

i ran away to the forest
and waited for that one tree
to fall so i could hear it

when she wanted to be
a savior of my snowcapped heart
i climbed the steep passages
and found her in a cave
waiting for me

soldiers
you are the brave

the swastika burns
in the fires of hell

nobody wants to admit that
the rain makes things
feel brand new again

but i know that the wet ground
will bring the flowers
i have been waiting for for so long

Lightning

butterfly sting
a wasp is the last one
to know what has happened to it

dancing churches
christ bled
and my eyes do too

a bump on my chin
it is a pimple
it is a leftover scar
from chicken pox

clear the mind of all clutter
she is a he
with a deep voice
with whiskers growing on
his face

what about the sex?
is it good?
how do they do it?

the sky billows safe tears
the sun hides from the fear
of lightning and thunder

Not Ugly

hot rod stomach ache
fingers coated in tears
all alone and together

feel the throbbing in my chest
my heart is a dormant volcano
i want you to wake it up

no worries no worries
the pimple on her cheek
does not make her ugly

goblins beat the horses
eat them
throw away the bones

uneven eyebrows
or a unibrow
frida kahlo was hot

lonely fears
i am a disc being thrown
into the air

Appearances Can Be Deceiving

arms wet from the rain
ouch!
the drops of blood dripping
like melting ice

teeth yellow
nose blue
eyes on fire

a deep breath
come to me death
i am waiting

the collar on the shirt
is stiff
like a green banana

hallelujah!
i am the luckiest
person in the world

please refrain from chewing gum
in class
pop pop pop

where the life is easy
where the sun makes you
into a brown nut

Can It Be That Difficult?

cancer of the mind
it erodes and erodes
until there is nothing left

hunger of the stomach
growl growl
it accepts anorexia

the happy man
makes people laugh

the angry woman
makes people blush with
her off color words

if one day you have
a heart attack then you
may see god

or you may live in
fear of the next one

beware the times
when the darkness is complete

there is a werewolf waiting
in your bed

Jack

the man with the oval face
tried to capture the moment
when he became handsome

the mirrors lied
he was a sinner
he was a faker

a goose walked by him
he kicked at it
it honked back in disapproval

the dog shit he stepped in
smelled like a meth head's breath

finally he took a knife
and made a jack-o'-lantern
on his face

there now
i am ugly
nobody will want me

i will never fall in love
i will never have sex with
a beautiful woman

Problems

pressure on the cheeks
a bee in his ear
chocolate melting in his warm mouth

there was a bullet
still lodged in his side
it only hurt when it got cold

they married on a saturday
at city hall
they kissed on the steps

a cat roamed in the streets
during the night
catching a mouse or two

the clock was broken
he threw it across the room
to get more sleep

greasy palms
teeth full of plaque
a donkey heehaws down the hill

red apples
green bananas
ocean spray cranberry juice

The 20's

they danced all night long
and the night was turning into day
when they finally went home

she poured a glass of vodka
it was 8 am
he wanted it so badly

the cigar he smoked
made the room like a typical
day in los angeles

they sat on the couch
remembering the early days
when they would make love
with the stars twinkling in their eyes

she sighed
and put her forearm to her forehead
i can't think anymore she said

he rubbed her shoulders
he kissed her neck
but she drew away like
a page being turned in a book

this is it
you will not stay here any longer
goodbye goodbye

Adolescence

the pimples on his face
look like stars that have
turned pink and red

chin up
whiskers down
hair greased up
and ready to be lit

bottle of cold heineken
a roast beef sandwich

what does that have to do
with why you hate me?

you stole the toothpaste
you broke the toilet
you ate the last of the vanilla ice cream

run run run
run around the front yard
in your socks

those callouses will not
bother you for another
hundred years

How Embarrassing- Paying For Sex

that's all i need
a pack of cigarettes
and a fifth of whiskey

when i watch television
and swallow my whiskey
it feels like i'm dancing
in my underwear

the light off
the candles burned
and the glow of the end
of my cigarette
keeping me company

where is she?
she should have been here by now
the money still fresh
from the atm

i pace back and forth
thinking about the times
i wasn't with her
how lonely i was

she was the only woman
i knew
the rest of my friends were gay men

Steve Baba is a poet and writer living in San Francisco. He has 9 poetry collections published, and has a short story collection forthcoming. Steve likes to relax in deserted cafes and likes to reminisce about his times in NYC, Santa Fe, New Mexico, Honolulu, Hawaii, and his ubiquitous time in Merced, CA.

www.ingramcontent.com/pod-product-compliance
Lightning Source LLC
Chambersburg PA
CBHW061733020426
42331CB00006B/1222